WOMEN OF FAITH™
STUDY GUIDE SERIES

UNDERSTANDING
PURPOSE

BY

CAROLYN
CUSTIS JAMES

FOREWORD BY

SHEILA WALSH

THOMAS NELSON
Since 1798

NASHVILLE   DALLAS   MEXICO CITY   RIO DE JANEIRO

✦Acknowledgements✦

Special thanks to my husband, Frank; Judy Nelson; Milli Jacks; Alexis McElhinney; Amy Lauger; Robert, Erik, and Andrew Wolgemuth; Lori Jones; and the many friends who prayed.

Published in Nashville, Tennessee, by Thomas Nelson. Thomas Nelson is a registered trademark of Thomas Nelson, Inc.

Thomas Nelson, Inc. titles may be purchased in bulk for educational, business, fund-raising, or sales promotional use. For information, please email SpecialMarkets@ThomasNelson.com.

Published in association with the literary agency of Wolgemuth & Associates, Inc.

Unless otherwise noted, all Scripture quotations are taken from *The Holy Bible*, New International Version®. NIV®. © 1973, 1978, 1984 by International Bible Society. Used by permission of Zondervan. All rights reserved.

Scripture quotations marked NLT are taken from *The Holy Bible*, New Living Translation, © 1996. Used by permission of Tyndale House Publishers, Inc., Wheaton, Illinois 60189. All rights reserved.

Scripture quotations marked GNT are taken from *The Holy Bible*, Good News Translation in Today's English Version—Second Edition. © 1992 by American Bible Society. Used by permission.

Scripture quotations marked MSG are taken from *The Message* by Eugene H. Peterson, © 1993, 1994, 1995, 1996, 2000, 2001, 2002. Used by permission of NavPress Publishing Group. All rights reserved.

ISBN: 978-1-4185-0711-4

Printed in the United States of America
HB 06.30.2020

✦CONTENTS✦

✦ FOREWORD ✦

*God knew what he was doing from the very beginning.
He decided from the outset to shape the lives of those who love
him along the same lines as the life of his Son.*

— Romans 8:29 MSG

Over the last ten years, as I have traveled across America
with Women of Faith, I have had the opportunity to speak to
over three million women in conferences across the nation.
Our conference theme changes each year—it may be grace,
hope, or faith—but the central message is the same: God sees
you just as you are, he loves you just the way you are, and he
has a purpose for you.

At these conferences, I have had the pleasure of talking
to many of the women that I meet at my book table, and I've
joyfully discovered that I am not alone in my quest to find
out what on earth God had in mind when he created Eve, the
very first woman. Now there is an influential woman!

Before Adam and Eve sinned, they would never have
questioned their purpose. Their lives were consumed with
loving God and each other. They were living the purpose of
every man and woman ever created. But when sin entered the
world, so too did questions, the most primal of all being: What
is my purpose? Why am I here?

Even for those of us who love God, we often question what our purpose is. Perhaps that is because we have
confused purpose with what we do, as opposed to who we
are. When God walked and talked with Adam and Eve, the
delight they all experienced was in the relationship—not in a
long list of tasks well done.

One of the legacies of sin is that we all experience a vacuum inside. Even in our best moments, there is a sense that there has to be more. This is the distant memory of Eden, as deep as the marrow in our bones. Our natural tendency, particularly as women, is to try and fill this void with doing something. Even if we are already over-committed, we try and fit in one more thing and end up worn out. Living a life of purpose may require all we have, but it is not intended to leave us burned out, dissatisfied, or feeling far away from God.

Perhaps we also question our purpose, imagining that if we were living it, there would be no sense of frustration and weariness at times. Christ came to restore our humanity, but we still live in a fallen world. Until we see him face to face, we will all experience moments of pain and sadness. So how then do we define a life of purpose?

As you begin this study, it is my prayer that you will catch a glimpse of the depth of God's love for you and that you will joyfully embrace the true purpose of every woman—to love God with all we have and are and allow that love to overflow to others.

God bless you!
Sheila Walsh

✦ INTRODUCTION ✦

DOES ONE SIZE REALLY FIT ALL?

In 2002, the subject of purpose became a headliner with the release of Rick Warren's book, *The Purpose Driven Life.* The book broke all sorts of sales records, skyrocketing to the bestseller list where it held its place at the top for months. Men and women everywhere, both young and old, had their noses buried in this book, searching for answers to one of the most basic questions a human being can ask — *What on earth am I here for?* In Atlanta, even a desperate fugitive from the law stopped long enough to listen as his hostage, Ashley Smith, read aloud to him portions from Rick's book, putting "purpose" in the headlines again.

Our study narrows the focus from this wider search for our purpose as human beings to ask another question — *What is God's purpose for me as a woman?*

To be honest, this isn't always the easiest topic for us to discuss. Raise the subject of a woman's purpose, and you'll stir up all sorts of different reactions among women. Either we've heard it all a hundred times before and wonder why we should bother going over it all again, or, for one reason or another, our lives haven't followed the accepted blueprint, and we dread getting left out of the conversation one more time. Still others of us cherish our out-of-the-mold lives and aren't about to risk engaging a discussion that may cause us to feel guilty about the choices we've made.

All of these reactions strike a chord within me. I grew up in a Christian home believing that God created me to be a wife and mother. That's what my parents taught me and that was the message I heard from the church. In my heart of hearts, I believed this was God's purpose for me as a woman and I wanted it more than anything. Then I got left behind.

Instead of getting married after college, I entered a ten-year stretch of unintended singleness. And when I did finally marry, I faced a painful battle with infertility. During those years, God opened doors for me I never anticipated, both in ministry and in my career. I discovered gifts and abilities I never knew I had or expected to use. To my surprise, I felt a deep sense of fulfillment in spheres I never imagined entering.

God used those unexpected experiences to take me deeper in my relationship with Him. He also used them to shake me up and cause me to ask new questions about His purpose for me as a woman.

Is God's purpose for us too small? Does it only fit some of us and then only for certain seasons of our life so long as everything holds together? We want to fulfill His purpose for us, but so often, it just seems hopeless. Does God have a purpose that is big enough for all of us? Or are some of us doomed, like Cinderella's stepsisters, to be forever trying to squeeze into a pair of shoes that simply don't fit?

If you're feeling that sense of dread, let me begin by reassuring you that this study is intended for you. Our goal is to make sure no woman is left behind. We have a great God, and His purposes are big enough to include every one of us—from our first gasp of air to the day we breathe our last. His purposes celebrate our uniqueness. After all, He created us. He delights in our diversity and intends for us to flourish no matter what shape our lives take. He is also wise enough to anticipate the snags, tragedies, and heartaches we experience, too, and has built into His blueprint the kind of flexibility that life in a broken world demands.

Rest assured. You have nothing to lose and a whole lot to gain from this study. By sticking together as we study, plenty of surprises are in store. Best of all, this study gives us a fresh opportunity to discover anew God's great heart for His daughters. That alone makes this discussion worth the effort.

After going through this study, one young woman, who brought a lot of hurt and apprehension to her search for purpose, reflected with relief and joy, "For the first time, I feel like I have wings!"

I pray that through this study you'll discover God gave you wings too.

CHAPTER 1

FINDING MY PURPOSE IN A BROKEN WORLD

"I CRY OUT TO GOD MOST HIGH, TO GOD WHO WILL FULFILL HIS PURPOSE FOR ME."

Psalm 57:2 NLT

At seventeen, Joni Eareckson's heart was filled with dreams and her whole life stretched out before her. Surrounded by friends, this bright, talented, promising young woman exuded life. The future was hers for the taking, and she was ready to spread her wings and fly. That was before her fateful dive into the lake that summer. Her head hit a tree stump concealed in the dark waters, and the impact broke her neck. She was grounded for life, as paralysis took her body hostage. There would be no flying now. How does talk of purpose fit into a story like Joni's?

One sunny Florida day in October 1999, three happily married women in Orlando kissed their husbands goodbye and all three men boarded a Learjet bound for Texas. These couples had been through this routine a hundred times before, but this time would be different. That night, the same three women crawled into bed in a torrent of grief, after the plane crash that turned them into widows. What happens to a woman's purpose when events take such a tragic downturn?

Dreams were reality for author and speaker Carol Kent. She had a strong marriage and a flourishing ministry. To top it off, her only child was a constant source of pride and joy. Jason graduated from the U.S. Naval Academy and as a young lieutenant was on his way to a promising career. The question on Carol's lips was, "Does life get any better than this?" Then came the shattering phone call, informing her of her son's arrest for murder, and Carol's whole life collapsed. Can a woman's purpose survive when everything she's prized and worked to build stands in utter ruins?

That's the way it is with life. Things may be going well. You may be enjoying luxuries and success, prestige and power, good health and prosperity. Then storms roll in with sudden vengeance, and your ship begins to sink.

—Thelma Wells

Our lives are not all the same, and we do not all follow the same path. For some of us the path looks a lot like we hoped, and we are finding rich fulfillment at home, in the workplace, or in a blend of both. But sometimes a life-altering crisis reconfigures our lives, destroying tender hopes we've cherished since we were little girls. Many women's lives appear at a standstill because marriage, children, the dream career, or financial success simply hasn't happened. Perhaps we feel that we've made such a mess of things ourselves that we've lowered our expectations to Plan B or something less.

Dreams can be illusive, but we all have them. We make plans too, yet our plans are fragile, no matter how realistic and careful we are. We live in a fallen, broken world, where anything can happen and where we drink deeply of our own brokenness. Plans collapse. Dreams slip from our grasp when disappointment, catastrophe, bad choices, and roadblocks of all sorts put them out of reach. But God has a vital purpose for His daughters.

1. As we begin this study, what do you believe is a woman's purpose? Where do you believe a woman finds her greatest fulfillment and why do you believe this to be true?

*J*udging from the stories of the five women we've discussed and the kinds of setbacks and losses we all experience in our lives, understanding purpose in a fallen world seems to put us on shaky ground, doesn't it? There are so many "what ifs" that can cheat us out of life's best for us.

2. What are the "what ifs" in your life? What changes or adversities might make it difficult (or impossible) for a woman to achieve her purpose as you have defined it above?

3. What has happened to you or to someone you love that seemed to put purpose out of reach?

*S*urprisingly, the Bible tells the truth about the fallenness of our world and our own hearts, yet doesn't give the slightest hint of shakiness when it comes to God's purposes for us.

Isaiah the prophet lived during a dark time in Israel's history, when everything was falling apart and there were more reasons to despair than to hold onto hope. Isaiah looked away from the chaos around him to the God who rules over heaven and earth, and his confidence revived.

4. **Read Isaiah 46:9–10 and Psalm 33:10–1.** What does God want us to know about Him and about His purposes?

5. How does today's news or a sense of your own brokenness affect your outlook on your life? How can we be certain that God's purposes will withstand the pressures of a fallen world? Why?

6. King David speaks of God's purposes in a more intimate way. **Read Psalm 57:2 and 138:8**. What hope did David have of purpose when he was in trouble, surrounded by enemies bent on destroying him? How does this speak hope to your own heart?

*T*he Bible tells us that our plans and purposes may fail, but God's purposes never will. Not the ups and downs of life, the wickedness of others, our failures and mistakes, the tragic reversals of life, nor the strongest powers in heaven or on earth, can destroy God's purpose or force

Him to adjust His plans. I find that deeply encouraging, don't you?

King Nebuchadnezzar of Babylon (today's Iraq) had a different problem with purpose. He was overconfident in his own purposes and his ability to carry them out. "Is not this the great Babylon I have built as the royal residence, by my mighty power and for the glory of my majesty?" (Daniel 4:30).

God brought Nebuchadnezzar down to size by turning him out of his throne room and causing him to lose his sanity, leaving him to eat grass along with the beasts of the field. Nebuchadnezzar's sanity returned when he lifted his eyes to the heavens and acknowledged his dependence on God.

7. Read Nebuchadezzar's words in **Daniel 4:34–35, 37.** What did Nebuchadnezzar learn about God's purposes, and why should this reassure and comfort us?

8. **Read Psalm 139:13–16.** How detailed are God's purposes for you?

od's people have always banked upon a God who is in control and whose purposes are sure. Broken necks or broken wings, crashing planes and beloved children who go astray—add whatever you like to the list—*nothing* can stand in the way of God's purposes for us. We are in His hands and His purposes are advancing in our lives, here and now.

I can never lose my purpose as a woman. God's purposes for me are indestructible, even in a broken, changing world.

✦DIGGING DEEPER✦

King David drew great comfort when he realized God's purposes for him extended down to the everyday details of his life. Read Psalm 139 to discover and reflect on how intimately God is involved in the details of your life and on how much you and your purpose matter to God.

✦PONDER AND PRAY✦

The lives of Joni, the three widows, and Carol Kent were permanently reconfigured by the tragedies they suffered. In a single day, their dreams and plans went up in smoke. The pain of their losses still remains with them today. But God's purposes for each of them (as well as for their loved ones) survived intact. In the words of one of the grieving widows, "Even when you hit bottom, there's still a rock to stand on."

God will not allow anything to interfere with His good purposes for His children, nor does He accomplish His purposes for one child at the expense of another. Because He is God, He is big enough to do this. There is great mystery to the way God works, but these women all draw strength and courage from the fact that their lives are in God's hands and that He is accomplishing His purposes for them.

As you reflect upon God's great and certain purposes, ponder this thought: *How does it change my prayers to know God's purposes for me are so secure?*

✦LOOKING AHEAD✦

Since God's purposes never fail, our study to understand our purpose is truly promising. We want our lives to count. We'd like to make a difference. So what is God's purpose for us as women? Our search for answers takes us back to the beginning of time, where God created the woman and cast a vision large enough to include all His daughters.

> *God wastes nothing. Not our joys, not our sorrows—nothing.*
>
> –Nicole Johnson

✦ Notes & Prayer Requests ✦

CHAPTER 2

FINDING MY PURPOSE WITH A LITTLE HELP FROM OPRAH

"SO GOD CREATED HUMAN BEINGS IN HIS OWN IMAGE. IN THE IMAGE OF GOD HE CREATED THEM; MALE AND FEMALE HE CREATED THEM."

Genesis 1:27 GNT

Every year, pollsters conduct surveys to determine the most admired women of the year. Oprah Winfrey frequently tops the lists. Women admire Oprah for her courage and determination in overcoming tremendous odds to become one of the most amazing success stories today. We respect her intelligence, talent, and hard work. Warmth, compassion, and straight talk are her trademarks. Remarkably, she's used her success to make a difference in the lives of many people. Little wonder she keeps appearing on our most admired women list.

But many women don't stop with admiring Oprah. They want to be *like* her!

1. If you believed your purpose in life was to become the next Oprah Winfrey, what would you do to make sure you reached your goal?

- Try to imagine what she is really like
- Read a book about Oprah
- Never miss the Oprah show
- Subscribe to "O" Magazine
- Talk to someone who has met her
- Google "Oprah" on the Internet
- Pose as a reporter and land an interview
- Meet her in person
- Shadow her to observe and study her ways
- Attend one of her live shows
- Get to know her best friend
- Spend time with her
- Become her best friend

Turn the tables now. How would obstacles disappear if all of this was Oprah's idea, and she wanted you to become the next Oprah Winfrey? What doors would she open to make sure you knew her well enough to represent her authentically and accurately to others?

Our search to understand a woman's purpose begins with God. He created us and holds the secrets of our purpose, so we can be sure He will give us whatever we need to fulfill our purpose.

Let's get the big picture first.

2. Genesis 1 describes creation. On days 1–3, God creates the spheres or environments and on days 4–6, He creates the inhabitants of each sphere. Read the passage and list in the first two columns what God created on each day *before* He created people. We'll come back to column three shortly.

Environment	Inhabitants	Purpose
Day 1: Genesis 1:3–5	**Day 4:** Genesis 1:14–19	
Day 2: Genesis 1:6–8	**Day 5:** Genesis 1:20–23	
Day 3: Genesis 1:9–13	**Day 6:** Genesis 1:24–31	

3. As God creates, He also defines purpose for everything He makes. Review verses 14–25. List in column three above the purposes God assigns to the inhabitants of each sphere.

4. In a steady rhythm, God follows the same basic process over and over again as He creates the world and its inhabitants. If you were a reporter observing these unfolding events, how would you summarize what God is doing?

*Y*ou may have heard the creation story a hundred times, but this time, stop and drink in the drama.

On day 6, God abruptly halts the action. He wants to grab our attention. Something major is about to happen. In the pause, we go behind the scenes to overhear God—Father, Son, and Holy Spirit—pouring over plans for the creation of the human race. The plan He unveils is a complete surprise.

5. **Read verses 26 and 27**. What does God say? What is God's design for the man and the woman He is about to create?

his is *God's* idea. He made Himself the pattern. He chose us to be like Him and to represent Him in this world. This is the first and most important fact a woman can know about herself and her purpose. It ought to take our breath away.

6. How does this change how you see yourself? The value of your life and the significance of your actions? Your relationships with others? Can you imagine a higher calling?

7. How should our identity as God's image bearers transform how we value, respect, and treat one another? How does this cast a vision of what we are to become?

> *I was in God's mind before I was ever in the womb of my mother. Specific attention, thought, and planning took place about me before God actually formed me in the womb.*
>
> —Marilyn Meberg

8. Returning to our original Oprah example, as God's image bearer, what do you need most to help you reflect Him more authentically? What incredible doors did God open to you when He said, "Let's make her to be like Us"?

- - - - - - - - - - - - -

Purpose 1: God created me to be His image bearer.

- - - - - - - - - - - - -

*G*od created you to be like Him. Before you were born, He wired into your DNA the necessity for a relationship with Himself. This is true of every woman. We are His representatives in this world — His eyes and ears, His voice, His hands and His feet. He wants people who interact with us to get a taste of what He is like because of our character and how we treat them. It is a sober responsibility, an awesome privilege. There is no higher calling.

✦DIGGING DEEPER✦

"Image bearer" language runs all through the Bible. Here are a few examples. Look up the verses below and consider the following: What attribute does God call us to reflect? What reason does God point to in Himself that stands behind this calling? I'll answer the first one to get you started.

	Attribute	Image-Bearer Reason
Leviticus 19:2	holiness	for I, the Lord your God, am holy
John 17:21		
Ephesians 4:32		
1 John 4:19		

As you read your Bible, be on the lookout for this image bearer theme.

✦PONDER AND PRAY✦

What person do you know best? Your husband? Your best friend? Do you know God as well as you know them?

The Old Testament describes God's people as those who walked with God. "Enoch walked with God" (Genesis 5:22, 24); Noah "walked with God" (Genesis 6:9). God called Abraham to "walk before me and be blameless" (Genesis 17:1). Abraham was "God's friend" (James 2:23).

We were created to know and walk with God—to journey with Him through life, enjoying His friendship, seeing the world though His eyes, loving what He loves and joining His cause. When we walk with God and learn to imitate His ways we are reaching toward our true purpose as women.

✦Looking Ahead✦

We have learned that a woman's first and highest purpose is to be God's image bearer—to know and become like Him. We share this purpose with men. The second aspect of our purpose, however, centers specifically on us as women. You may want to buckle up, for the next part of our study is sure to surprise you!

"You have made us for yourself, O Lord, and our hearts are restless until they find their rest in you"

—St. Augustine

CHAPTER 3

FINDING MY PURPOSE AS A DAUGHTER OF EVE

"THE LORD GOD SAID, 'IT IS NOT GOOD FOR THE MAN TO BE ALONE. I WILL MAKE A HELPER [*ezer*] SUITABLE FOR HIM.'"

Genesis 2:18

"Excuse me — I don't want to be inquisitive — but should I be right in thinking that you are a Daughter of Eve?"

In C.S. Lewis' classic book, *The Lion, The Witch and The Wardrobe*, a faun named Mr. Tumnas addresses those memorable words to Lucy, a young girl who has just arrived unexpectedly in Narnia. She has come, so the story goes, by way of the wardrobe stationed in the spare room of the old professor's house where she and her siblings were guests. By addressing Lucy as a "Daughter of Eve," Mr. Tumnas stumbles upon a core truth shared by all women. We are, without exception, Daughters of Eve.

However, this label comes with a good deal of negative baggage. A friend of mine told me she cringes every time the subject of Eve comes up. I think a lot of us feel that way. After all, Eve is blamed for bringing down the whole human race, when she disobeyed God by eating the forbidden fruit, and giving some to her husband as well. We'd like to avoid a shameful legacy like that.

In Narnia, however, the arrival of a Daughter of Eve is welcome news. Lucy's presence poses a deadly threat to the dark powers that hold Narnia and all its inhabitants in the icy grip of winter.

1. How do you feel about being called a Daughter of Eve? What positive and negative impressions do you have of Eve?

*E*ve may not make our "Most Admired Women" list, but she wins first prize for being the most influential. Like her or not, we can't ignore her if we want to understand our purpose. God cast the mold for women when He created Eve. Her creation is central to understanding our purpose.

Genesis 2:4–25 provides more details about day six, when God created male and female in His image. Events in this passage took place between Genesis 1:25 and 31.

2. Read the passage. Three different voices make statements about the woman. Identify each speaker and what they say about her.

	Who is speaking?	What does he say about the woman?
Genesis 2:18		
Genesis 2:23		
Genesis 2:24		

3. The word "good" appears seven times in Genesis 1 (verses 4, 10, 12, 18, 21, 25 and 31). What problem does God identify in Genesis 2 that disrupts this repetition? How concerned does God appear to be?

God tells us that He knew us in our mother's womb. He tells us that He knows us, even better than we know ourselves. And best of all, He knows something beyond what we know: He knows what He is calling us to become.

—Nicole Johnson

4. What do you think was actually wrong? What did the man need? Do you think all men share Adam's need? Why or why not?

5. How did God make Adam aware of his need? What solution did God propose and how did God describe His solution?

6. How do the words of the man and the words of the writer of Genesis (Moses) honor the woman? What do they imply about the nature of their relationship and how important the woman is to the man?

*I*n verses 18 and 20, two Hebrew words describe the woman. Each word carries a lot of meaning, so it's important to stop and study a little Hebrew before we move on. (Don't worry. You're going to love this!)

Here are the two words:

Hebrew Word	English Translation
ezer (pronounced with a long ā, as in "razor")	"helper," "help," or "strength"
kenegdo (pronounced kĕ-nĕg-dō — the first *e* is very short, like the first *e* in "sĕvere")	"meet" or "suitable"

Kenegdo only appears here in the Bible and means the woman is "in front of" or "corresponds to" the man. It establishes the fact that she is his match, his equal, his counterpart, his partner. As one Old Testament scholar put it, woman is to man "as the south pole is to the north pole." That's *kenegdo*.

Now let's look at *ezer*.

The *ezer* is one of the best-kept secrets in the Bible. We've gotten used to hearing *ezer* translated as "helper" or, when combined with *kenegdo*, sometimes as "helpmeet." Usually, we think of *ezer* is another word for wife, which is why so many women start feeling left out about now. While wives and mothers are certainly included, *ezer* encompasses a whole lot more.

In the Old Testament, *ezer* shows up 21 times as a noun. Here's the breakdown:

Number of Times	Used For
2	Woman
3	Nations Israel turned to for military aid
16	God, as Israel's help or helper

Because of this inventory, *ezer* was upgraded from "helper" to "*strong* helper." But there's more.

Whenever the word *ezer* is used in the Bible — for nations and for God — it appears in a military context. Israel appealed to these nations for military aid. God is our "shield and defense," "better than chariots and horses." The evidence indicates *ezer* is a military word. The *ezer* is a warrior!

Okay. Hebrew class dismissed. Now let's explore what this implies about us if God created women to be warriors.

7. Look back at your answer for question 4 to see if anything you wrote about what the man needed fits what a warrior might be called to do. What conditions call for a warrior? How was earth a fierce battlefield right from the start? What danger was lurking?

8. What battles has God called you to fight? How does being a warrior change your view of yourself and of your relationships with others?

*Purpose 2: God created me to be an
ezer-warrior for His cause.*

On learning God created her to be a warrior, one woman remarked, "I don't mind being called a 'helpmeet.' I love helping people. But *helpmeet* doesn't describe everything I am. *Warrior* does!"

Little wonder the evil powers of Narnia trembled. The daughters of Eve are warriors for God's cause—for our husbands, our children, our friends, neighbors and colleagues—wherever God stations us in the battle.

✦ DIGGING DEEPER ✦

"Warrior" language runs all through the Bible. Look up these New Testament verses and note how God calls us to be valiant warriors against the Enemy:

Romans 13:12

Ephesians 6:10–20

1 Peter 5:8

Romans 8:35–37

2 Corinthians 10:3–5

As you read your Bible, be on the lookout for this warrior theme.

✦ PONDER AND PRAY ✦

Under unbearable grief, Carol Kent faced her son's trial and sentencing like a true *ezer*:

> There's a huge part of my heart that wants my purpose to involve a positive outcome for my son. But I am not the author of the grand story God is writing. During this chapter of life, God's will for [my husband] Gene and me is that we join Him now in what He wants to accomplish through the process of today's suffering. Our perspective is changing as we realize we are in a spiritual battle here on earth, and we are called to be warriors.
> —taken from *When I Lay My Isaac Down*

We're all in this battle. How good to know we are not alone! God is our *ezer*. He is with us. He is for us. And the Enemy is no match for Him.

✦ LOOKING AHEAD ✦

Our understanding of our purpose is growing. We are God's image bearers, created to know and walk with Him. We are *ezer*-warriors, fighting for God's purposes no matter where God puts us. In our next study, we will explore God's vision for the relationship between the man and the woman.

✦ Notes & Prayer Requests ✦

CHAPTER 4

FINDING MY PURPOSE ON GOD'S A-TEAM

GOD BLESSED THEM AND SAID TO THEM,
"BE FRUITFUL AND INCREASE IN NUMBER; FILL THE
EARTH AND SUBDUE IT. RULE OVER THE FISH OF
THE SEA AND THE BIRDS OF THE AIR AND OVER EVERY
LIVING CREATURE THAT MOVES ON THE GROUND."

Genesis 1:28

My husband and I were having dinner one evening with a young man who had successfully dodged the marriage altar for years. He'd had some close calls and left a string of broken hearts along the way, yet somehow, he always managed to escape. But his current relationship was different, and he knew his Houdini days were over. There'd be no escaping marriage this time.

As he confided to us about the woman who had captured his heart, he began to contemplate the future. Deep in thought, he mused, "You know marriage is a lot like a three-legged race. It's uncomfortable, unnatural, and takes some getting used to. In fact," he added philosophically, "it's like learning to walk all over again."

His words reflected a fairly pessimistic view of marriage, one we did not share. But he had some pretty strong evidence to support his point. The "battle of the sexes" is not a foreign idea to any of us. We hear jokes about it all the time. But it is no laughing matter when it surfaces in marriage, the workplace, or the church. Sometimes relationships between men and women do hobble like a three-legged race. And sometimes they are even worse.

1. How does this image of a three-legged race make you feel? Draw from your own experience to describe a situation where relationships between men and women fit this description.

*T*he Bible doesn't share this three-legged view of relationships between men and women. God views these relationships as a Blessed Alliance. When He had a big job to do, the team He put together for the job was male and female. In Genesis 1:27–28, we learn that after God created "male and female" in His image, "He *blessed* them" (emphasis added) and then gave them their global mission. We are God's A-Team. We enjoy God's special blessing, and His image in us shines brighter, as we join our brothers in serving Him.

Let's take a closer look as God spells out the details of our purpose. We'll backtrack a little to Genesis 1 and day six of creation.

2. **Read Genesis 1:26–31** again. On the chart below, draw lines connecting the verses with what God is doing.

Bible Passage	What is God doing?
Genesis 1:26	Providing for the physical needs of His creatures
Genesis 1:27	Evaluating creation and pronouncing it all "*very good*"
Genesis 1:28	Revealing His plan to create male and female in His image
Genesis 1:29–30	Creating male and female as His image bearers together
Genesis 1:31	*Blessing* His image bearers and unveiling their global mission

3. From Genesis 1:26–31, how much territory and what spheres of life are involved in our purpose?

4. Judging from the staggering scale of this enterprise, what workforce is required to tackle such an assignment? What team did God choose?

5. Today, how do we continue to fulfill our mission to be fruitful and multiply, to rule and subdue?

6. If these creation commands are only physical (to populate the earth and to manage the earth's resources), are we leaving out any women? Explain. Considering the entire span of your lifetime, during what seasons of your life are you left out?

> *You might appear to be different—or even strange—to some people. But remember, God made you in His image for His glory. Use your uniqueness to edify people and glorify God. Capitalize on the abilities God has given you.*
>
> —Thelma Wells

ur purpose involves these physical callings, but is also profoundly spiritual. In Matthew 28:18–20 Jesus calls us to reproduce *spiritually*, by making disciples and to rule and subdue by spreading His kingdom—His justice, compassion, and righteousness—throughout the whole earth.

The Blessed Alliance zeroes in on the marriage relationship and the home, but expands beyond that to the wider world. God intended for men and women to join in serving Him in every sphere of life. There's no trace of a three-legged race here.

7. The Bible gives strong examples of godly women and men working together in all sorts of contexts—raising families, working the land, building and defending cities, prophesying, leading, governing, and even engaging in battle. What examples do you recall from your Bible reading of men and women joining forces for God? How did the Blessed Alliance succeed or fail?

8. How does the Blessed Alliance change how you feel about the men in your life—your husband, brothers, friends and co-workers? What opportunities do you have to align with them in battling the Enemy and advancing Christ's kingdom?

Purpose 3: God created me to be a vital member of the Blessed Alliance.

✦DIGGING DEEPER✦

"Blessed Alliance" language runs all through the Bible. Jesus wants His followers to unite together in love and interdependence. Look up the verses below and notice how much we need each other.

John 13:34–35

John 17:11, 20–23

Romans 12:4–8

Ephesians 4:1–6

Philippians 2:1–4

As you read your Bible, be on the lookout for this Blessed Alliance theme.

✦ PONDER AND PRAY ✦

For all but three years of his life, C. S. Lewis was a confirmed bachelor. During his three years of marriage, he discovered the importance of the Blessed Alliance and gained a new appreciation for why "It is not good for the man to be alone." After his wife died of cancer, Lewis wrote this tribute to his beloved *ezer*:

> For a good wife contains so many persons in herself. What was [she] not to me? She was my daughter and my mother, my pupil and my teacher, my subject and my sovereign; and always, holding all these in solution, my trusty comrade, friend, shipmate, fellow-soldier. My mistress, but at the same time all that any man friend (and I have good ones) has ever been to me. Perhaps more. . . . Did you ever know, dear, how much you took away with you when you left?
>
> —taken from *A Grief Observed*

✦ LOOKING AHEAD ✦

So how do these purposes fit into our lives? How do we go about becoming better image bearers or equipping ourselves as warriors? We have such different personalities, circumstances, and gifts. Maybe we're not all cut out for this. In our next study, Jesus takes two very different women (some think polar opposites) and guides them gently, but firmly down the very same path to pursue their purpose as women.

CHAPTER 5

Pursuing My Purpose at the Feet of Rabbi Jesus

"There is really only one thing worth being concerned about. Mary has discovered it—and I won't take it away from her."

Luke 10:42 NLT

The Brothers Grimm included in their repertoire of fairy tales, the story of Snow White and Rose Red—two sisters who were as different from each other as night and day. One was energetic and adventuresome, while the other possessed a quieter and gentler disposition, preferring to remain at home.

Moms with more than one child often remark on how different their children can be from one another in personality, interests, and gifts. Of course, for parents this means what you learned in parenting your first child doesn't necessarily work on the second or the third.

In New Testament times, the sisters Mary and Martha were not exactly two peas in a pod either. Mary was the quiet, reflective type who repeatedly got into trouble by stepping outside the sphere in which a woman in her culture was expected to remain. Her big-hearted older sister Martha was a woman of action and words. She had a passion for serving others and a readiness to speak her mind. Sadly, these two women have become icons of differences we observe among ourselves. We tend to divide ourselves up into "Marys," women who like to think, study, and learn, and "Marthas," women who care about people and love to serve.

> *The wonder of it all is that the Lord can use everything for whatever purposes he chooses. Not to mention everyone.*
>
> —Patsy Clairmont

What makes these two sisters particularly fascinating and relevant to our study is their friendship with Jesus. We meet up with them three times in the Gospels for wonderful glimpses into Jesus' relationships with two very distinct women. But as we revisit their story, we discover that Jesus calls us to become a composite of the two—women who learn *and* women who serve. I hope you'll notice that the Bible doesn't tell us their demographics—age, marital status, children, or occupation. That gives each of us permission to see ourselves in their stories.

1. What differences (backgrounds, families, circumstances, gifts, interests, etc.) exist among the women in your study group or circle of friends? How are you unique from one another?

2. Read **Luke 10:38–42.** This is where we meet Mary and Martha for the first time. Based on this passage, how would you describe the two sisters' different personalities? Which sister do you identify with most? Why?

3. Education for women in Mary's day was extremely rare. Rabbis in Jesus' day frowned upon teaching women because they believed women lacked the mental ability to learn. Keeping this in mind, briefly describe in your own words what happened in Mary's and Martha's encounter with Jesus.

4. Luke doesn't tell us what Jesus was teaching Mary. Based on Jesus' deep conversations with other people, what do you think Jesus was teaching her?

nd consider this interesting tidbit. In the original Greek text, Luke (who also wrote the book of Acts) describes Mary "sitting at the Lord's feet" and Paul the apostle "sitting at the feet of Gamaliel" (Acts 22:3, some English translations say "under"). This language identifies both Mary and Paul as rabbinical students. Clearly Jesus was teaching Mary the same deep truth He taught His male disciples. Mary was engaged in serious learning.

5. Why did Martha object? Can you relate to her frustration? Why or why not?

6. How would you feel if thirteen hungry men (including Jesus) showed up at your house? Considering the culture's views of women at the time, how would you expect Jesus to respond to Martha?

7. When Jesus defends Mary, He makes a strong statement about a woman's purpose. What does He say? Why do you think Jesus felt so strongly about Mary's choice? What is He telling Martha about the choice she is making for herself?

*O*nce again, Oprah helps put things in perspective. If your main purpose in life was to know and become like Oprah Winfrey, and Oprah dropped by and was sitting in your living room, what would be the best way for you to pursue your purpose? By going to the kitchen to prepare a meal or by joining her in the living room?

8. So how does Jesus' answer point both Mary and Martha to their purpose? Why is He so emphatic? What message is He sending Martha? What message is He sending you?

I pursue God's purpose for me by taking time and making the effort to know Jesus better.

✦DIGGING DEEPER✦

Among your relatives and friends, what person knows and understands you best of all? What have they done, differently from other people, to become so close to you?

Jesus desires that same kind of understanding and urges us to get to know Him better. What could be more important than investing time and effort to understand the One who made us, who holds our lives in His hands and who calls us to trust Him as we journey through life?

The apostle Paul couldn't agree more. See Philippians 3:7–21. When he was chained in a Roman prison cell, having lost his freedom and every comfort, his possessions, his career, and potentially his life, what did Paul and Mary share in common?

Do you hunger to know God better? He created you for this! According to Jesus, nothing is more important than taking time to know Him.

✦PONDER AND PRAY✦

Knowing about God is crucially important for the living of our lives. . . . We are cruel to ourselves if we try to live in this world without knowing about the God whose world it is and who runs it. The world becomes a strange, mad, painful place, and life in it a disappointing and unpleasant business, for those who do not know about God. Disregard the study of God, and you sentence yourself to stumble and blunder through life, blindfold, as it were, with no sense of direction and no understanding of what surrounds you. This way you can waste your life and lose your soul.

—J. I. Packer, *Knowing God*

Jesus is God's true image bearer and our perfect role model. He came to show us the Father—"everything about him represents God exactly" (Hebrews 1:3 NLT). As you read and ponder God's Word, ask Him to open your eyes to know Jesus better.

✦LOOKING AHEAD✦

Tough battles lay ahead for both sisters, as they do for us. Vital as it is to sit at the feet of Jesus, this is only the beginning. In the next study, Jesus continues teaching Mary in a very different and painfully difficult setting.

✦ Notes & Prayer Requests ✦

CHAPTER 6

PURSUING MY PURPOSE IN THE TRENCHES

"LORD, IF YOU HAD BEEN HERE, MY BROTHER WOULD NOT HAVE DIED."

John 11:32 NLT

On the morning of September 11, a woman was sitting at her desk in the South Tower of the World Trade Center, ready to start another day of work. When the first hijacked plane plunged into the North Tower, terror rushed through her veins. Without a second to lose, she dashed to the exit and began her panicked descent—all 102 floors—racing to get out of the building alive.

As she and thousands of others were escaping, a courageous stream of rescue workers was pouring in—NYC fire fighters and police, along with a few brave volunteers—heroically and deliberately risking their lives to save total strangers trapped inside. Even when they felt the buildings shake and knew their time was short, they refused to abandon the people they had come to save. I hope we never get over sacrifices like that.

How reassuring to know that when we're in trouble and dial a desperate 911, these kinds of committed and courageous people will come to our aid.

But when Mary's brother Lazarus was dying, and she and her sister Martha dialed a frantic 911 for Jesus, they didn't get a quick response. Instead of dropping everything and racing to His friend's sickbed, Jesus delayed two whole days before heading to Bethany. By the time He arrived, it was too late. Lazarus was dead. The funeral was over. Mary's faith in Jesus was shaken to the core, and her purpose was slipping away.

1. Can you relate to Mary's struggle with Jesus? How have you experienced a similar situation where God didn't do what you expected? What kinds of questions were you asking about God?

I am not an afterthought. All God's love-inspired preplanning for each of us is not haphazard or impersonal. His timing may throw me or His sovereign plan may grieve me, but I am always sheltered in His sovereign hand.

–Marilyn Meberg

2. Read the story of Lazarus' death in **John 11:1–37**. What did Mary believe about Jesus that led her to count on Him in this crisis? Why did she expect Jesus to come quickly to help them?

3. How did Jesus respond differently than she expected? What did Jesus actually do?

4. If you had been the puffy, red-eyed Mary, going out to meet Jesus who arrived on the scene too late to save your brother, what would be your state of mind? What would you be thinking and feeling about Jesus? What would you expect or want to hear Him say?

5. Given the fact that Jesus already knows He is going to resurrect Lazarus, does it surprise you that He weeps? Why or why not?

6. What does this tell you about how He views you when you are struggling and don't understand what He is doing?

Through this crisis and Mary's struggle to trust Jesus in the messiness of life, she will learn more about Jesus than if she only sat at His feet and listened. It is one of the great mysteries of life, that God does some of His best work in us when we are struggling the most. Circumstances may be careening out of control. But Jesus never loses control, and His purposes for us move forward, even in the chaos.

7. What did Mary learn about Jesus *before* He raised her brother from the dead? What was Jesus revealing about Himself through her disappointment in Him? What are you learning about Jesus through your struggles?

8. How was Rabbi Jesus teaching Mary to trust Him even when He didn't do what she expected? What does Mary's encounter with Jesus teach us about how Jesus is working through our struggles to build a stronger relationship with us?

I pursue God's purpose for me
by going deeper with God in the
hard places of my life.

✦ DIGGING DEEPER ✦

The Bible contains story after story of circumstances when God's people are disappointed with Him and wrestle to understand His delays and silences. The life of faith isn't easy.

Can you hear your own voice in Psalm 10:1 and 13:1–2? Troubles drive us to God with honest questions that open the door to a deeper, more authentic relationship with Him.

When Jesus arrived in Bethany, Martha told her sister, "The Teacher is here." Martha was right. Whether we are studying in the school of Rabbi Jesus or wrestling in confusion, "The Teacher is here"—teaching us more about Himself, deepening our faith in Him, making us stronger warriors for His cause.

✦ PONDER AND PRAY ✦

All of us have heartache in our lives, times when God could have fixed things, but He didn't. Yet even in these hard places, we are making progress.

God never wastes pain. He always uses it to accomplish His purpose. And His purpose is for His glory and our good. Therefore, we can trust Him when our hearts are aching or our bodies are racked with pain.

—Jerry Bridges, *Trusting God*

✦ Looking Ahead ✦

Some may think there are two kinds of women—the Marys and the Marthas. But Jesus calls us to be both—to think and learn about Him and to translate our knowledge into compassionate ministry to others. Mary is about to prove that point.

✦ Notes & Prayer Requests ✦

✦ Notes & Prayer Requests ✦

CHAPTER 7

PURSUING MY PURPOSE ON THE FRONT LINES

"SHE HAS DONE A BEAUTIFUL THING TO ME."

Mark 14:6

When my daughter Allison was twelve, she and I traveled to Oregon so I could support my mother, who was facing major surgery to remove a tumor. I never imagined I would need support too. While I joined my dad at my mother's bedside, Allison joined a group from my parent's church for a bike trip.

The surgery went badly. Instead of relieving my mother's pain, it ignited a new pain that was simply off the charts. For days after my mother came home, my dad and I were up with her through the night, phoning the surgeon, begging God to help, dispensing narcotics, frantically trying whatever we could to relieve her pain. It was a nightmare. I've never seen anyone suffer like she did.

Between episodes, I fell into bed, soaking my pillow with tears over my mother's agony and my helplessness to stop it. I think my dad was doing the same. The battle raged on after

Allison returned. One terrible night as I slipped back into bed (trying not to awaken Alli who was sleeping next to me) and lay there in tears, I felt her arm go around my neck. I can hardly describe the comfort and strength that flowed from her love to me.

I think Jesus must have felt something like that when, as He contemplated the Cross, Mary reached out and ministered to Him. Burdens are eased and hearts are soothed when a woman pursues her purpose.

1. Describe a time when you were struggling and someone unexpectedly reached out to you, or how you felt when no one noticed and you carried your burden alone?

2. **Read John 12:1–8** and describe the setting of this event. Where were they gathered? Who was there? When did this event occur? What was the occasion?

3. What lay ahead for Jesus and how do you think the spirit of festivities clashed with how He was feeling that night? How was Jesus alone?

4. This was a gathering of men reclining at the table. Women could serve, but were expected to remain in the background. Instead, Mary created a spectacle. What did Mary do?

> *We can take our eyes off ourselves and our own journey and realize that this is a group outing— that we are not supposed to arrive in heaven alone but hand in hand.*
>
> –Sheila Walsh

5. How did Jesus' disciples respond and why did they think Mary was making a big mistake? Do you think their words wounded Mary? Why or why not?

> *When Jesus realized what was going on, he intervened. "Why are you giving this woman a hard time? She has just done something wonderfully significant for me. You will have the poor with you every day for the rest of your lives, but not me. When she poured this perfume on my body, what she really did was anoint me for burial. You can be sure that wherever in the whole world the Message is preached, what she has just done is going to be remembered and admired."*
>
> —Matthew 26:10–13 MSG

6. How did Jesus respond and how did Jesus interpret Mary's actions? See **Matthew 26:12.** Did Jesus think she knew what she was doing?

7. What do His words suggest about how deeply she had ministered to Him?

8. How do Mary's actions reflect her purpose? How is she imitating Jesus? How does she enter the battle with Jesus and encourage Him to fulfill His purpose? How does Mary help you see your own calling to enter the sufferings of others?

I pursue God's purpose for me by entering the sufferings of others.

✦ DIGGING DEEPER ✦

Here are some extraordinary examples of God's people standing together on the front lines of the battle:

Exodus 17:9–12

Ruth 1:16–17

1 Samuel 20:13

Esther 4:14

Philippians 1:3–5

As you read your Bible, notice how much God's people need each other. It's not good for any of us to be alone.

✦PONDER AND PRAY✦

When we honestly ask ourselves which per-
sons in our lives mean the most to us, we often find
that it is those who, instead of giving much advice,
solutions, or cures, have chosen rather to share
our pain and touch our wounds with a gentle and
tender hand. The friend who can be silent with us
in a moment of despair or confusion, who can stay
with us in an hour of grief and bereavement, who
can tolerate not-knowing, not-curing, not-healing
and face with us the reality of our powerlessness,
that is the friend who cares.

—Henri Nouwen, *Out of Solitude: Three*
Meditations on the Christian Life

✦LOOKING AHEAD✦

God calls his *ezers* to stand with others on the front lines of
the battle. We can easily see our purpose in these crucial
moments. But what about the little things we do that go
unseen? Does our purpose include the mundane things
we do for others every day? In our next study, we'll turn
to Martha to explore how we pursue our purpose behind
the scenes.

CHAPTER 8

Pursuing My Purpose behind the Scenes

"Martha served..."

John 12:2

Anna had a gift for noticing the hurt look in a person's eyes. Her spiritual antennas were always rolled out in search of someone who needed a friend. Adults and teenagers found in her an attentive listener, a safe confidant, and a caring heart. She used her culinary skills to gain entrée into situations where other approaches wouldn't work. The elders in the church often shook their heads in amazement at how often they arrived on the scene of a crisis, to discover she was already on the job.

She never stepped up to the podium or felt the warmth of the spotlight. There was no applause for what she did, no "fifteen minutes of fame." She transported the elderly to countless medical appointments and helped them balance their checkbooks. She had honest heart-to-heart talks with kids, which is why they loved her. She was a behind-the-scenes kind of person, and she didn't crave the limelight. Still, one wonders if her purpose was as significant as people who were out in front.

1. Describe an unsung hero or heroine you know. What do you think this lack of recognition implies about the true value of their work?

*I*f Martha had a competitive streak in her, being the sister of Mary of Bethany wasn't easy. Mary, who always did the right thing. Mary, whose actions always earned public praise. It isn't easy to be an unsung hero, but that's what Martha was. Truthfully, we're like Martha most of the time—working behind the scenes, doing all sorts of ordinary things no one ever notices.

For Martha, things were even worse. Not only were her contributions largely hidden, her honest reactions—and legitimate concerns—kept getting her into trouble. And we are usually very hard on Martha for her mistakes.

2. **Read Luke 10:38–42** from Martha's point of view and jot down ways the story focuses on her.

3. There's no indication that Martha was fussing over place cards, flower arrangements, and fancy hors d'oeuvres. This was an incredible opportunity to serve Jesus. She simply wanted to do her best. If Jesus and His disciples arrived on your doorstep, hungry and tired, what would you do? Why does Martha's complaint to Jesus make a lot of sense?

4. How would you feel if you were Martha, and Jesus said to you, "Martha, Martha, only one thing really matters. Mary has found it, and I won't take it away from her"? How would you respond?

> *The Creator has made us each one of a kind. There is nobody else exactly like us, and there never will be. Each of us is his special creation and is alive for a distinctive purpose. Because of this, the person we are, and the contribution we make by being that very person, are vitally important to God.*
>
> –Luci Swindoll

5. How are Jesus' words an invitation to Martha, rather than a rebuke? Why did Martha need to sit at Jesus' feet, just as much as Mary did?

If I could say only one thing, it would be simple and to the point: God knows all about you. He knows your good days and your bad days. He knows the noble thoughts and the shameful thoughts. He sees your devotion and your indifference. And he loves you—totally, completely, passionately, boundlessly. Forever.

–Sheila Walsh

6. Jesus' purpose for Martha also involved wrestling with hard questions. Read Martha's encounter with Jesus in **John 11:5–6, 17–28.** In this brief conversation, Martha shows herself to be as deep and thoughtful as her sister Mary. How does Jesus call Martha to trust Him in the painful present and how does she move from doubt to faith in Him? Do you relate to Martha's battle to trust Him? Explain.

7. **Read John 12:1–3.** The last time we see Martha, she is back in the kitchen again. How is this dinner gathering similar to the one in Luke 10 where Mary sat at Jesus' feet and how has Martha changed? How does she act differently?

8. What parts of your life are lived "behind the scenes"? How do you feel if you're relegated to the kitchen, when all the big things seem to be happening in the other room? How does Martha's example help you see purpose in everything you do—whether you're in the spotlight or working unobserved behind the scenes?

I pursue God's purpose for me behind the scenes, in the little things I do.

✦Digging Deeper✦

Hagar is another behind-the-scenes person in the Bible. No one cared about Hagar. This insignificant slave girl appears briefly as an extra in the bigger, more important stories of Abraham and Sarah. Yet God met Hagar in a face-to-face encounter when she was fleeing for her life. Hagar was His image bearer. God had a purpose for insignificant, unwanted, invisible Hagar.

Hagar named God *El Roi*—"the God who sees me" (Genesis 16:13).

No image bearer is insignificant. Everything we do matters. Jesus even notices when we take a cup of cold water to a little one in the middle of the night (Matthew 10:42). Anything we do in His name, as His follower, matters!

What difference does it make to know that God's eye is on you and that you matter this much to Him?

✦Ponder and Pray✦

In Frances Hodgson Burnett's beloved English novel, *The Secret Garden*, the young orphaned Mary Lennox stumbles upon the lost key to an untended, but once beautiful, walled garden on her uncle's grand estate. At every opportunity (and beneath the radar of any adults), the little girl regularly makes her way to the garden where she covertly works and lovingly tends the long-neglected garden.

When her uncle, wanting to ensure her needs were met and she was happy, asks her if she wants anything, her request is simple. "Might I have a bit of earth?"

God has given each of us "a bit of earth"—a territory entrusted to us where He calls us to represent Him and to advance His kingdom. Our sphere of influence can be our husband and children, the workplace, the wider community, a close circle of schoolmates, or our friends. I know a woman whose "bit of earth" is an extended care facility where she is a resident. No matter where God puts us, we have kingdom work to do.

What is your "bit of earth"? What people has God put in your life? What battles does He call you to fight for Him?

✦ LOOKING AHEAD ✦

In the next four lessons we will look more closely at the arenas where God calls us to fulfill our purpose as image bearers and ezer-warriors. We will examine the lives of women who are role models for us in living out God's purposes for us in our world today.

✦ NOTES & PRAYER REQUESTS ✦

CHAPTER 9

LIVING MY PURPOSE IN THE HOME

"I KNOW THAT YOU SINCERELY TRUST THE LORD, FOR YOU HAVE THE FAITH OF YOUR MOTHER. . . AND YOUR GRANDMOTHER. . ."

2 Timothy 1:5 NLT

The familiar adage "the hand that rocks the cradle rules the world" pays fitting tribute to the powerful influence of mothers. A mother's stamp of influence on her child—for better or for worse—is difficult to erase. Many a queen mother has had her finger in world affairs by influencing a son or daughter who occupied the throne. But even ordinary citizens like the rest of us cannot escape the influence of our mothers. The home is a crucial sphere where we live out God's purpose for us as women.

I have vivid memories of trudging home after school in my teenage years and having long talks with my stay-at-home mom. She was a great listener and she let me talk until I had no more to say about my day. My daughter and I carried on the tradition and dubbed it the "data dump". Even now, though my mother and I live in opposite corners of the country (Oregon and Florida), I love to pick up the phone and have a good long talk with her.

But my mother did more than listen. She also taught me a lot and passed on many things she no doubt learned from her mother. In the process, she exerted a powerful influence on me, as a woman and as a Christian. Even today, when I'm faced with a difficult situation, I reach for the theology I learned from my mother.

Not every mother/daughter relationship is a good one. Some women even grow up without ever knowing their mothers. In any case, mothers leave their mark on us, and we live daily with the impact of that relationship or its absence.

1. As you think about your relationship with your mother, how has she impacted your life, for better or for worse?

*S*amuel would have joined this discussion. He owed a lot to his mother, for he always carried with him the wise theology he learned from her. Hannah learned about God, not in a theological seminary or a local Bible study, but from her intensely personal battle with infertility.

2. Read **1 Samuel 1.** Hannah's story opens with the family tree, just waiting for her to add the next branch. She was Elkanah's first wife, but she failed to conceive—probably for several years. As you read, allow yourself to feel her agonizing monthly disappointments. Some of us know from personal experience exactly how she felt. If you were Hannah, how would you react to the disappointments, pressures, and family dynamics she faced in her battle with infertility? How did it feel to have another woman bear children for her husband?

"What the mother sings to the cradle goes all the way down to the coffin."

Henry Ward Beecher
(1813–1887)

3. Elkanah's love for Hannah was strong, but that didn't diminish her pain. Why did his words and gestures of love, intended to cure Hannah's sadness, fail to comfort her? How would his comment make you feel if you were Hannah?

4. Notice how often God is mentioned in the first eight verses. His actions are stated as simple facts, but they take us to the heart of Hannah's struggle. What was God doing and how did that make Hannah's situation even worse? How do you relate to her struggle with God? How do you think she felt about her purpose as a woman? Explain.

5. If the LORD prevented Hannah from conceiving, what was He doing for Peninnah? How might Peninnah's attitude change if she understood God's goodness to her?

"I learned more about Christianity from my mother than from all the theologians of England."

John Wesley (1703–1791)

6. Although Hannah didn't know it, God was preparing her for a major role in Israel's history—one she accomplished simply by raising her son. Though Peninnah's barbs were unbearable, they brought out the warrior in Hannah. Where did Hannah go with her pain and how far was she willing to go to vindicate God's honor?

7. Read Hannah's prayer in **2 Samuel 2:1–11**. How would you feel if you were about to part with your precious child? With little Samuel nestled close by her side, what is the spirit of Hannah's prayer? How are Hannah and Samuel a Blessed Alliance for God's purposes in Israel?

8. What does Samuel hear his mother say about God's rule over human lives as she prays? How do her words reveal the truth about God's hand behind the ups and downs of your own life?

*H*annah's teachings lodged in Samuel's young heart. As an adult, he would use his mother's theology as he mentored Israel's first kings. Hannah's theology—what she believed about God—formed the bedrock of Israel's theology and continues to influence Christians today.

God entrusts mothers and mentors with strategic opportunities to shape the faith of the next generation of God's people. And the theology we teach comes from what we learn about God as we wrestle with private heartaches and find Him worthy of our trust.

I live God's purpose for me as a woman by advancing His kingdom in my home.

✦DIGGING DEEPER✦

Originally the book of Samuel was written as a single book. But it was too long to fit onto a single scroll and was therefore divided into 1 Samuel and 2 Samuel. This two-volume work opens with Hannah's psalm and closes with King David's psalm (2 Samuel 22). Read David's psalm and look for traces of the theology that passed from Hannah to her son to the heart of the king.

✦PONDER AND PRAY✦

A high school teacher in a Christian school tirelessly pumped her students full of God's Word. One of her students took it all in, but never took it to heart. He became a successful businessman and a regular churchgoer, still keeping God at arm's length. Then, just as he was nearing his retirement, everything fell apart. His company failed. Heartbreaking problems broke out in the church. Stress and anxiety robbed him of sleep, and his wife feared it would kill him. One sleepless night, as he tossed in bed, the verses started coming back—one after another. God's Spirit worked in his heart, and a soul was brought to life.

God's purposes advance through mothers and mentors who are fruitful and multiply true image bearers. Lives are at stake in our efforts. The impact of our influence goes far beyond what we can see. History offers ample proof that God works in powerful ways when *ezers* invest themselves in their children. There's no telling what He will do through us!

✦ LOOKING AHEAD ✦

We are passionate about our homes and our families. But we are also passionate about the church. How are we *ezers* in the church? We'll explore that subject next with some unexpected help from the apostle Paul.

✦ NOTES & PRAYER REQUESTS ✦

CHAPTER 10

LIVING MY PURPOSE IN THE CHURCH

"... WE ARE ALL ONE BODY IN CHRIST, WE BELONG TO EACH OTHER, AND EACH OF US NEEDS ALL THE OTHERS."

Romans 12:5 NLT

*I*f you passed her on the street, you'd certainly notice her flamboyant hat—a trademark of this remarkable woman. But you'd probably never guess she was a woman of enormous influence, a warrior in the church.

You may have never heard of Henrietta Mears. She's been gone for over forty years, but it's fairly certain you've been impacted by her ministry through Christian leaders she once taught in her Sunday school class. As young people, Bill and Vonette Bright, co-founders of Campus Crusade for Christ International, and the great evangelist Billy Graham all sat under her teaching. Rev. Graham later remarked, "I doubt if any other woman outside my wife and mother has had such a marked influence [on my life]. She is certainly one of the greatest Christians I have ever known!"

Henrietta was a woman of purpose. She never married, but she was remarkably fruitful in her teaching ministry. She multiplied exponentially in young lives. She had a passion for God's Word and poured it into the hearts of others. She is just one of countless women—past, present, and future—who invested their lives and gifts to build up the body of Christ. Those who come under their godly influence and benefit from their wisdom rise up and call them blessed.

1. What women in the church have had a strong impact on you and how have they benefited you?

*I*t may come as a surprise to some, but the apostle Paul (originally known as Saul of Tarsus) shared Billy Graham's enthusiasm and gratitude for the gifts and ministries of women. He actually planted the first church in Europe with the help of women. Before we dive into their story, let's take a closer look at Paul.

2. Paul was a man's man—an authentic Jew, with the pedigree to prove it. Read his credentials in Philippians 3:4–6 and Acts 9:1–5 and summarize his resume.

$\mathcal{P}$aul was on his second missionary journey through Asia Minor (today's Turkey) visiting fledgling churches he planted on his first journey when God disrupted his plans. Paul and his team tossed their itinerary, packed their belongings, and headed for Europe instead.

3. Read **Acts 16:6–40**. How did God disrupt Paul's plans? If you had been Paul, after all this fanfare, what would you expect to find when you reached Philippi (today's Greece)? How would you feel to arrive and find a group of women praying? What does this tell you about how important women are to God and to His church?

4. Who was Lydia and what dangers did she face in Philippi as a new believer? See **Acts 16:19–24 and 36–40**. What does her determination to host the church in her home (verses 14–15, 40) reveal about the risks she was willing to take to follow Christ? Does this kind of adversity fit your view of what it means to be a Christian? Why or why not?

*W*hat started as a women's Bible study blossomed into one of the strongest New Testament churches, clearly a favorite congregation of Paul's. Later, from a prison cell, Paul wrote a letter to the Philippians that sounds a bit like Billy Graham praising Henrietta. In Paul's opening lines he makes explicit reference to the founding mothers of the Philippian church who were there "on the first day."

5. **Read Philippians 1:3–5.** How did Paul regard these women and why did he value them so much?

*P*aul's letter reads like a war report—one soldier writing words of courage to fellow soldiers on a different front of the same war. He was in prison, possibly on death row. The Christians at Philippi faced hostility and violence. The Enemy was working, and there were battles to fight. Paul is talking about purpose—teaching us how to fulfill our purpose as women in the church.

6. **Read Philippians 1:27–30.** Paul counted on *ezers* to stand with him in battle. In verse 30, he writes, "We are in this fight together" (NLT). What battles were Paul and the Philippians fighting? What battles has God called you to fight against the Enemy? What lives are at stake on your battlefront? What is Paul's counsel to you?

7. Image-bearer language runs through Paul's letter. He inserts a picture of Jesus in his letter for the Philippians to study and, not surprisingly, to imitate. **Read Philippians 2:3–11.** How does Paul portray Jesus and how does Paul practice what he preaches (see verses 17–18 and 3:8–11)? How would Jesus' attitude look in your life? How does this go against the natural grain of our hearts?

When we realize our days here matter, our pain has significance, and our choices are meaningful, we can step through the darkest of times with hope in our hearts. It's not that we don't waver, but even our inquiries have the potential, when we are seeking, to lead us to a stronger faith.

–Patsy Clairmont

8. Considering Paul's background, what made his strong alliance with Gentile women unlikely? What similar oil-and-water combinations exist in our Christian relationships today and how do our disagreements and broken relationships serve the Enemy? What advice does Paul give us to overcome our differences and unite together for the sake of Christ (see Philippians 1:27; 2:1–2; 4:1–3)?

I live God's purpose for me as a woman by using my gifts and ministries to build up the church.

✦DIGGING DEEPER✦

Every Christian is vital to the health and strength of the church. Paul uses the metaphor of a physical body to emphasize this point.

Read Romans 12:4–10. Think about your own body. What happens to you when any part of your body breaks down? Paul describes the church as the body of Christ. How do we make the body of Christ healthy and strong, or anemic and weak?

✦PONDER AND PRAY✦

The biggest surprise in the story of Paul and the Philippian church is the transforming power of the Gospel in Paul's personal life. Jesus didn't come simply to save our souls. He came to transform our relationships—to build a Blessed Alliance out of incompatible individuals. Based on his resume, Paul was the last person to send to Gentile women. But he was God's choice, and God's power was at work in his heart.

These women needed Paul. But Paul also needed them. Even for a single man like Paul, it was "not good for the man to be alone." God blessed him with an army of *ezers*, and he thanked God for them every time he prayed. His letter makes it abundantly clear that the whole church needs our gifts and ministries too.

✦ LOOKING AHEAD ✦

As our relationship to God impacts our homes and loved
ones, God's purposes for us as women ripple out and
spread beyond this intimate circle into the church. But the
ripple effect doesn't stop there. God has given us a global
purpose. We'll see that next, as we explore our purpose in
the world.

✦ NOTES & PRAYER REQUESTS ✦

CHAPTER 11

LIVING MY PURPOSE IN THE WORLD

"YOU ARE THE SALT OF THE EARTH. . . . YOU ARE THE LIGHT OF THE WORLD— LIKE A CITY ON A MOUNTAIN, GLOWING IN THE NIGHT FOR ALL TO SEE."

Matthew 5:13–14 NLT

hen Kay Warren read a magazine article about HIV/AIDS in Africa, her heart was gripped and broken at the thought of 12 million AIDS orphans in Africa. "I didn't know a single orphan," she admitted. But her passion for Christ trumped her excuses, and this self-described "white, suburban soccer mom" caught a global vision and made up her mind to get involved. Kay Warren is an *ezer*.

God called my friend Lisa to the corporate world. This Christian businesswoman is not only committed to excellence on the job—she also wants to be a light in the workplace by conducting her business God's way. In her interaction with colleagues and competitors, she is constantly asking image bearer questions such as, "What would Jesus do?" and the equally important, *"How* would He conduct Himself here?"

In 2005, *Forbes* ranked Condoleezza Rice first in their yearly survey of "The Most Powerful Women in the World." As

America's Secretary of State, this committed Christian is an *ezer* in the heady sphere of government and international affairs.

These women cast a wider vision for the many ways God calls women to fulfill their purpose in the world. Our mission as image bearers spans the entire globe, and while we can't all contribute in the large ways these women do, this worldwide vision is nevertheless included under the umbrella of God's purposes for women. As *ezer*-warriors, we are called to join our Christian brothers in every sphere of life, in the home, the church, and also to live as lights in the world, whether we're in education, a corporation, government, or missions. We rule and subdue by spreading justice, mercy, compassion, and honor in God's world.

1. What Christian woman—past or present—is your most-admired kingdom-builder in the public sphere and why do you admire her?

bigail's bold venture into the public arena was brief, but significant nonetheless. Her husband Nabal was a powerful man, the wealthy owner of large herds. The Bible makes no bones about how mean spirited he was, so we can only imagine what it was like for Abigail to be married to a man like that.

When Nabal selfishly provoked a political crisis, Abigail was pushed out of her comfort zone and into the public sphere. And like Kay Warren, she had no choice. She was compelled to act.

2. **Read 1 Samuel 25:1–38.** Abigail gets caught between two powerful men. Who were they? What was their relationship to her? From information found in this passage, describe their characters, moods, and what you think motivated them.

	Nabal	**David**
Who?		
Relationship to Abigail?		
Character?		
Mood?		
Motive?		

3. What hair-raising crisis did Abigail face? What terrible injustice was at the heart of the crisis and how was she caught in the middle?

How can we love God with everything and our neighbor as ourselves if we do not sacrificially give of ourselves with joy? In looking for the big opportunities to "perform" as a Christian, how many small God-given opportunities to love with depth do we miss?

–Sheila Walsh

*A*bigail powerfully illustrates a woman of faith living out her purpose in both the public and private spheres. She faces two hostile men in a sticky, volatile political situation. She rules and subdues by defending helpless members of her household who will lose their lives if she fails to act. She is also a wife dealing with her husband and a subject dealing with her king. Both men are on the wrong track — pursuing their own ends. Abigail boldly blocks her husband's evil actions and wisely turns the future king back to God. She is a strong role model for how women live out their purposes in relationships with men — in marriage, in the church, and in the world. She stands against injustice and evil. She offers godly counsel and promotes faith and obedience to God.

4. How did Abigail intervene between David and Nabal and why was this a dangerous mission for her? What frightening possibilities did she risk by coming between these two warring forces?

5. With the diplomacy of Condoleezza Rice, Abigail negotiated a peace settlement between an indignant David and her insolent, but absent husband. What would have happened to all parties involved if Abigail had remained passive? Can you see yourself acting boldly like this, or would you feel inclined to withdraw in this situation? How was God's honor at stake?

6. How did Abigail use her theology—her beliefs about God—to reason with David? And how did his response affirm her spiritual leadership in this situation?

The most wonderful truth behind dealing with distractions is that we don't need to organize and plan with our natural ability alone. The Holy Spirit, who gives us everything we need, can lengthen or shorten time depending on what He wants us to accomplish. If we yield ourselves to Him, He will order our steps according to his purposes.

—Thelma Wells

7. Imagine how you would feel (and what you would do) if you were Abigail, heading home to ill-tempered Nabal after undermining his refusal to grant David's request. What do Abigail's actions reveal about her spiritual backbone?

8. When God calls you to move out of your comfort zone—to take a stand, to initiate a difficult conversation, or to take up an important cause—how does Abigail's example encourage you to step out by faith to live God's purpose for you in the world?

I live God's purpose for me as a woman by being a light in my community, in the workplace, and in the wider world.

✦DIGGING DEEPER✦

"The fool says in his heart, 'There is no God.' They are corrupt, and their ways are vile; there is no one who does good" (Psalm 53:1)

Nabal means "fool" and accurately describes the man. Abigail's husband was created by God, lived in God's world, yet did not regard God in his thoughts or his actions. He was out of touch with reality and wasting his life. Nabal missed his purpose.

Abigail was no fool. She lived in God's world and she knew it. She speaks truth with grace. She advocated for others. This godly *ezer*-warrior lived for God's purposes by taking a stand and pointing others back to Him.

Not everyone is called to mediate a conflict between two powerful leaders, but all of us are called to be salt and light in the world. We bring the flavor of God's mercy and justice into a broken world that has forgotten Him. We bring the light of truth and the gospel to lost souls.

"For we are God's masterpiece. He has created us anew in Christ Jesus, so that we can do the good things he planned for us long ago" (Ephesians 2:10 NLT).

✦ PONDER AND PRAY ✦

We have to be braver than we think we can be, because God is constantly calling us to be more than we are, to see through plastic sham to living, breathing reality, and to break down our defenses of self-protection in order to be free to receive and give love. With God, even a rich man can enter the narrow gate to heaven. Earthbound as we are, even we can walk on water.

—Madeleine L'Engle, *Walking on Water:*
Reflections on Faith and Art

✦ LOOKING AHEAD ✦

I hope by now you've gotten a sense of God's large purpose for women. He makes plenty of room for all of us and His purposes enrich our lives with significance and meaning in the home, in the church, and in the wider world. Yet, when we contemplate our private lives, sometimes that largeness vanishes and our everyday world seems pretty small. Before we finish, let's go home and take another look at how we live for God's purpose on an ordinary day.

AWAKENING THE WARRIOR IN ME

**" . . . LET US THROW OFF EVERYTHING THAT HINDERS . . .
LET US RUN WITH PERSEVERANCE THE RACE
MARKED OUT FOR US . . .
LET US FIX OUR EYES ON JESUS . . ."**

Hebrews 12:1–2

The alarm beside my bed goes off. I will do today what I have done countless times before. Groan, of course, that my time to sleep is over and that yesterday's burdens and problems are here again. I reluctantly put my feet on the floor and head for the shower to begin another day. What does my day look like?

Unless something unforeseen happens, today looks just like so many others. I love the things I do, but they can be pretty ordinary and routine—clothes to wash, bills to pay, emails to answer, and dinner to figure out. I'll probably run an errand to pick up groceries and I'll interact with people I love.

Conversations with my husband are bookends on my day. We'll coordinate logistics—not as complicated now that our nest is empty—and talk about his work and mine, of life and struggles and what we are learning. Somewhere in my day, the phone will probably ring and my daughter, my mother, or my cousin will be on the line for another great "data dump." There's a pile of work on my desk, and another writing project waiting. At the end of the day, I'll leave a lot of unchecked items on my to-do list as I climb back into bed.

For all of us, most days have a certain kind of sameness about them. But they are anything but ordinary, for God is in our days, infusing them with purpose. We are God's image bearers and *ezers*. For us, every day is significant, every encounter is important, and so is everything we do.

1. For a moment, stop and encapsulate an ordinary day in your life — the people, activities, and challenges. What do you like best about your day and what do you dread most? How does it change things to know you to represent God and are a warrior for Him on the "bit of earth" He has entrusted to you?

*E*ach day brings fresh opportunities to live out our purpose. So, when we're forgetting our purpose, feeling overwhelmed, or just finding it hard to trust God and put one foot in front of the other, how do we regain our footing and find the strength to carry on?

The New Testament writer to the Hebrews believed it would help to compare ourselves to Olympic runners. As the runner's coach, he offers three pieces of advice, found in **Hebrews 12:1–2**. They provide a fitting conclusion to our study.

2. Enter his advice on the lines below. Then we'll unpack one at a time.

1. _____

2. _____

3. _____

3. In ancient Olympic Games, runners ran naked so nothing interfered with their running. (Evidently modesty and self-consciousness didn't slow them down!) In today's G-rated Olympics, what do modern runners do to ensure their running is unencumbered? What does the writer believe impedes us as we run the race of our lives? What are some examples of things that weigh us down?

Sometimes we search so hard for the miraculous that we miss the obvious reality of God's ever-present nearness.

–Patsy Clairmontt

4. Within the context of the letter to the Hebrews, the writer specifically targets unbelief, the sin that first brought down the human race. Sooner or later, most Christians struggle with unbelief—even mature Christians. How do you struggle to trust God and how does unbelief make it hard to pursue your purpose? How does knowing Jesus better help you throw off your unbelief?

5. What words does the writer use to describe the kind of effort and stamina we need to expend in living for Christ each day? What does this imply about the effort God wants you to invest in your purpose?

6. **Read Psalm 139:13–16** again. How did God's specific purposes for David comfort him? How does it boost your confidence to know your life is not an accident—that God has marked off your path and every step you take advances His good purposes for you, no matter what shape your life is in?

*I*n the 1992 summer Olympics, Britain's thirty-two-year-old Linford Christie won a stunning upset over younger competitors in the men's 100-meter race. He made an all-out effort, to be sure. But what caught everyone's attention was the half-crazed focus of his eyes. The London *Sunday Times* reported that Linford's "pop-eyed gaze made him look as if he was running from mortal danger rather than towards his finest moment."

7. What have you noticed about where Olympic runners focus their eyes and how that affects their performance? What does it mean to "fix your eyes on Jesus" and how is this possible when we can't actually see Him? What clues do Mary and Martha offer to help us understand what this means?

8. Did you notice that the writer doesn't talk to us as though we are solo runners? What traces of the Blessed Alliance do you detect in his words? How significant do you feel as you anticipate another day of living for God's purpose?

*I live God's purpose for me as a woman
every single day of my life.*

✦DIGGING DEEPER✦

The Bible gives us four versions of Jesus' story, told from the perspectives of Matthew, Mark, Luke, and John. Like a thick photo album, these men give us snapshot after snapshot of Jesus teaching, healing, caring for people, and living for His Father's purposes. Even after all of this, John threw up his hands and said, "Jesus did many other things as well. If every one of them were written down, I suppose that even the whole world would not have room for the books that would be written" (John 21:25).

The writer to the Hebrews urges us to "fix your thoughts on Jesus" (Hebrews 3:1).

As you read and study Jesus—in the Gospels especially—be asking yourself the question, "What does Jesus want me to know about Him from this?" and "What difference does it make for me to know this?" I think you'll be amazed at what you'll learn and how much you'll grow to love Him!

✦PONDER AND PRAY✦

A friend of mine recently floored me by announcing she had taken up motorcycling with her husband and young adult sons. But Adele wasn't just clinging to the back of her husband as he flew down the road on family outings. She had a 600-pound, high-powered motorcycle of her own. Furthermore, she rather enjoyed her new avocation as a biker, describing the experience as "quite a rush."

Something else she said intrigued me, as she discussed the hazards and safety issues involved in motorcycling. It seems that most learners take a spill or two before getting the hang of making a turn on the bike. The trick, she told me, is to "look where you want to go." Remarkably, the motorcycle always heads in that direction.

How is your story part of the great story that God is weaving throughout human history? Wherever God leads you, keep "fixing your eyes on Jesus." With Jesus as our focus, our study, our role model and friend, we'll stay true to our purpose no matter where our race leads.

✦A FINAL WORD✦

Whether we are young or old, married or single, busy at home or heading off to the workplace, raising our children, caring for an elderly parent, or requiring care ourselves, active in ministry or taking up an important local or international cause, God is working mightily in and through His daughters. He's drawing us into a deeper relationship with Himself. He's using our efforts on the front lines and behind the scenes to advance His glorious purposes.

We are His image bearers. We are His *ezers*. We are called to join our brothers in a Blessed Alliance serving our great God. My cousin summed it up perfectly as she reflected on God's great purpose for women: "The Bible is a gracious, spacious place for women."

I hope you feel that way too.

✦Leader's Guide✦

Each chapter begins with an illustration and an ice-breaker question intended to help the women in your group relax and join in the discussion. There isn't a "right" answer to any of these warm up questions, so everyone can participate without fear of giving a wrong response. Try to include everyone in this part of the discussion to help everyone feel comfortable and become involved in the subject matter.

Eight discussion questions guide you through the content of the chapter. When you pose one of these questions, be sure to give your group plenty of time to think and don't be surprised if they grow silent temporarily. This is fairly common in discussion groups, and the leader who gives the group ample time to reflect will find they will open up and talk. To help you stay on track, this guide identifies questions intended to draw out opinions and provides information for questions aimed at more specific answers.

The large, centered statement within each chapter states the main point of the chapter and corresponds to the **Focus** in the guide.

Digging Deeper is for those who want to do more thinking or digging in God's Word. This part is optional for discussion, but we hope you will want to go a little deeper in your study.

Ponder and Pray offers a great way to wrap up your study with thoughtful quotes from Christian leaders or additional thoughts for reflection and prayer.

Each chapter ends with a hint of what is coming in the next lesson which we hope will encourage everyone in your group to keep studying!

Chapter 1: Finding My Purpose in a Broken World

Focus: Purpose is illusive in a broken world. We long for purpose, but there are so many things that seem to spoil our purpose or put it out of reach. We're only chasing rainbows unless God holds everything together. Our purpose rests on the rock of God's unchanging character and His indestructible purposes.

1. to **3.** These icebreaker questions identify your starting point—what you already think about your purpose as a woman and what could cause you to lose it.

4. Isaiah and the psalmist reassure us that God is in control. If this were not true, we could never count on having a purpose.

5. These things can make us fear that we will lose our purpose. But our purpose is secure because God's purposes never fail, no matter what happens.

6. God doesn't require a perfect world or perfect people to accomplish His purposes. Nothing—not our sins, mistakes, failures, tragedies, the actions of others, or the devil's fiercest assaults—can stop God or throw Him off. What rich comfort this is for us.

7. King Nebuchadnezzar, the most powerful man on earth, was humbled to see his empire look so small compared to God's powerful reign. In response, Nebuchadnezzar drops to his knees and worships the King of kings.

8. Notice how intimately God has already been involved in your life. See how much you matter to Him.

✦Digging Deeper✦

Psalm 139 is loaded with statements that show God's intimate involvement with you. David's words are intended to bring the comfort of God's love to our hearts. Let these words remind you just how much you matter to Him and how He has planned every day of your life.

Chapter 2: Finding My Purpose with a Little Help from Oprah

Focus: The Bible opens with the earthshaking news that God created us to be His image bearers. We want to catch God's glorious vision for us and revel in the fact that He wants a relationship with us.

1. The example of Oprah helps us grasp the tremendous honor and challenge it is to be God's image bearer. God is giving us an extraordinary invitation to enjoy a relationship with Him.

2. to **3.** The God who made us defines our purpose.

Environment	Inhabitants	Purpose

Day 1:
  Genesis 1:3–5
light
(day and night)
	Day 4:
	  Genesis 1:14–19
	sun, moon, and stars
		–to serve as signs marking
		  seasons, days, and years
		–to give light to the earth
		–to govern the day and night
		–to separate light from darkness

Day 2:
  Genesis 1:6–8
sky
(separated from water)
	Day 5:
	  Genesis 1:20–23
	birds and fish
		–birds to fly
		–to be fruitful and increase in
		  number according to their kind
		–to fill the seas and the earth

Day 3:
  Genesis 1:9–13
land and plant life
	Day 6:
	  Genesis 1:24–31
	animals and human
	beings
		–land to produce plant life and
		  living creatures
		–living creatures to produce
		  according to their kind

4. Reporters don't bog down with details, so just summarize the highlights. God creates, defines, assigns purpose, then evaluates His work and pronounces it good.

5. God announces His plan to make men and women to be like Himself. Your Bible translation may use "man" in verses 26 and 27, but a better translation here is "mankind" or "human beings" since both male and female are included.

6. For starters, this means we inherited qualities from God—intelligence, morality, spirituality, love, compassion, mercy, creativity, a capacity for relationships, etc.—that give us dignity, meaning, and worth. It's impossible to come up with a complete list, because God cannot be reduced to a list. This also establishes a fundamental equality among all people.

7. God's image bearers have enormous significance and value, and we express our love for Him by honoring and caring for others. He calls us to the highest possible standard when He calls us to pattern our lives after Him.

8. God delegated the earth to us. He calls us to rule and care for it as He would. To understand who we are and *how* He would do things, we need to know Him well. When He created us to be His image bearers, He opened the door for us to enjoy a close relationship with Himself.

✦DIGGING DEEPER✦

	Attribute	Image-Bearer Reason
Leviticus 19:2	holiness	for I, the Lord your God, am holy
John 17:21	oneness	as Father and Son are one
Ephesians 4:32	forgiving	as Christ forgives you
1 John 4:19	love	because Christ loved us

Chapter 3: Finding My Purpose as a Daughter of Eve

Focus: God created women to be ezers—*a term loaded with astonishing implications for women. We are warriors for God's purposes all the days of our lives.*

1. Despite our mixed feelings about Eve, she is central to our purpose.

2.

	Who is speaking?	What does he say about the woman?
Genesis 2:18	God	The man's aloneness is not good. He **needs** the one I will create.
Genesis 2:23	Adam speaks poetry	He identifies with her—she is bone of my bones and flesh of my flesh—and gives her a name like his.
Genesis 2:24	Moses (narrator)	The man forsakes father and mother to be united to his wife, and the two become one flesh.

3. God is concerned enough to halt the narrative and deal with the problem before Adam notices anything is wrong.

4. This is an opinion question, although it is important to note that God's statement about Adam applies to all men. God created all of us for relationships with others. This doesn't only apply to married people. Singles share this deep need for close friendships too.

5. As Adam names the animals, it dawns on him that he is the only human being. God will make a "helper suitable" for the man.

6. Adam realizes she is part of him and rejoices in their union that goes to the bone—in flesh, heart, and purpose. Generations later, Moses surely shocked his readers by saying the man forsakes his family to unite with his wife. In the ancient culture, the wife left her family and was absorbed by her husband's clan.

Ezer verses:

- **Woman**—Genesis 2:18, 20

- **Nations**—Isaiah 30:5; Ezekiel 12:14 and Daniel 11:34

- **God**— Exodus 18:4; Deuteronomy 33:7, 26, 29; Psalm 20:2; 33:20; 70:5; 89:19 [translated 'strength']; 115:9, 10, 11; 121:1, 121:2; 124:8; 146:5; Hosea 13:9

7. Even before God created Adam and Eve, battle lines were drawn and the Enemy was planning his first attack.

8. God calls us to battle for His purposes in the lives of others.

✦DIGGING DEEPER✦

Romans 13:12	put on the armor of light
Ephesians 6:10–20	put on the whole armor of God
1 Peter 5:8	be self-controlled and alert, because of your enemy
Romans 8:35–37	we are more than conquerors
1 Corinthians 10:3–5	put on the armor of light

Chapter 4: Finding My Purpose on God's A-Team

Focus: God's view of a Blessed Alliance between men and women sounds a hopeful note and guides us to seek strong relationships with the men in our lives.

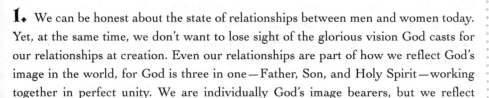

1. We can be honest about the state of relationships between men and women today. Yet, at the same time, we don't want to lose sight of the glorious vision God casts for our relationships at creation. Even our relationships are part of how we reflect God's image in the world, for God is three in one—Father, Son, and Holy Spirit—working together in perfect unity. We are individually God's image bearers, but we reflect God's image most brightly when we join together in serving Him.

2.

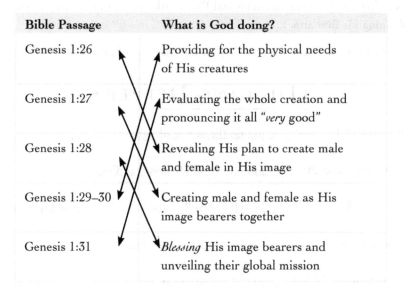

Bible Passage	What is God doing?
Genesis 1:26	Providing for the physical needs of His creatures
Genesis 1:27	Evaluating the whole creation and pronouncing it all "*very* good"
Genesis 1:28	Revealing His plan to create male and female in His image
Genesis 1:29–30	Creating male and female as His image bearers together
Genesis 1:31	*Blessing* His image bearers and unveiling their global mission

3. The whole earth is encompassed in our purpose. The home, the workplace, the entire planet. God's image bearers rule the earth as His vice-regents.

4. God's A-Team is both male and female. God's image shines most brightly in the world when men and women join forces for Him. Men and women need each other — not just in marriage, but in every setting.

5. God's mandate has occupied the human race since the beginning of time. We have populated the earth. God gave us an enormous ball of raw material. Just look at all we have made from it. We continue to explore, cultivate, protect, and utilize the earth's resources.

6. We're leaving out women who don't have children, or are physically unable (too young or too old or disabled) to rule and subdue the earth. But God's purposes include all of His daughters, from little girls to the elderly, regardless of our physical condition.

7. Here are some examples: Abraham and Sarah followed God's call to leave their homeland, but failed to encourage each other to trust Him in Sarah's agonizing struggle with infertility; Moses, Aaron, and Miriam (siblings) led the children of Israel out of Egypt, but their alliance collapsed when Aaron and Miriam became jealous of their brother; by faith, Rahab risked her life to aid the Israelite spies, and they, in turn, took action to rescue her and her family when Jericho was destroyed; Hannah prepared her son Samuel to become one of Israel's greatest leaders when she taught him deep truth about God; Mordecai called his cousin Queen Esther to risk her life for the sake of God's people, and her bold actions resulted in Mordecai's rise to power and influence in the Persian kingdom.

8. This is an opinion question. As you answer, remember the Bible's message that men and women need each other.

✦DIGGING DEEPER✦

John 13:34–35	Jesus' followers love one another.
John 17:11, 20–23	Jesus prays for us to be one as He is with His Father.
Romans 12:4–8	We are members of one body and each one has a job to do.
Ephesians 4:1–6	Paul calls us to unity in Christ.
Philippians 2:1–4	Humility, gentleness, patience, and love build our unity in Christ.

Chapter 5: Pursuing My Purpose at the Feet of Rabbi Jesus

Focus: The heart of our purpose as women is found in a relationship with Jesus. According to Jesus, knowing Him matters most in all of life.

1. Our differences reveal our great God's amazing creativity.

2. The writer intentionally contrasts the two sisters, so be sure to notice their differences.

3. Step inside the story, picturing the natural reactions and tensions among the people involved. Keep the ancient culture in mind to feel the shock of Jesus' reply.

4. Jesus with Nicodemus (John 3:1–15), the Samaritan woman (John 4:1–30), the grieving Martha (John 11:20–28). Jesus wasn't known for small talk. His mission was urgent, and He always took His followers deeper.

5. When men were gathered, women served and remained in the background. Martha objected because her sister belonged in the kitchen, not listening to Jesus with the men. Jesus' message for women is stronger because of the cultural setting.

6. This is an opinion question.

7. Jesus tells Martha that her sister Mary is doing the most important thing a woman can do—taking the time to know Him. Jesus knows that to trust Him, they need to know Him well.

8. Jesus is guiding Martha to her purpose as a woman. Both sisters need to know Him to fulfill their purpose and to face the treacherous road ahead.

✦DIGGING DEEPER✦

Paul echoes Jesus' words and reminds us that the main thing in life for all of us is to know Jesus for ourselves.

Chapter 6: Pursuing My Purpose in the Trenches

Focus: We pursue our purpose in the dark places of life. In suffering and loss, we cling by faith to what we know about Jesus, and He always takes us deeper.

1. Painful as this is, struggles and questions are necessary for a deeper relationship with God.

2. Jesus was on the other side of the Jordan River when Lazarus became ill. The only way to reach Him was to send a messenger to track Him down.

3. Mary has been Jesus' student. She has been working to know Him. In the crisis, she banks on what she knows of Him. Her urgent message to Jesus (John 11:3) contains clues of what she believed about Jesus that prompted her to seek His help. Find other clues in what people were saying about Jesus in this passage and why they couldn't believe He didn't come.

4. This is an opinion question.

5. Jesus' humanity was real. So were His tears. He genuinely grieves with Mary over Lazarus and the agonies death has brought to His world.

6. God's glory is inextricably linked to our good. His reputation is at stake in whatever happens to us. So even when we are suffering and don't understand, we can be sure He is working for our good and His glory.

7. Mary learns that Jesus doesn't always do what she expects; that even when she doesn't understand Him, she can trust Him. He knows what He is doing and He truly does love her. He doesn't scold her for falling to pieces, but affirms her pain by entering into her grief and weeping with her.

8. Notice Jesus deliberately delays. He is not confused. And because He loves her, He does not withhold this pain from Mary. He is leading her to a depth of faith that she will need when He faces the Cross. How does our faith grow stronger through our sufferings and disappointments with God?

✦ DIGGING DEEPER ✦

These psalms are meant for our encouragement. They remind us that even the strongest believers have moments of deep despair and struggle to trust God. We're in good company when we struggle to trust God and wrestle with hard questions about God. Even in these low moments, God is at work in our lives—teaching us and drawing us closer to Himself. I find that deeply encouraging, don't you?

Chapter 7: Pursuing My Purpose on the Front Lines

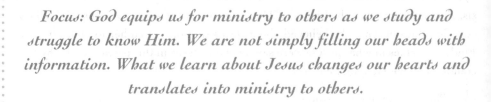

Focus: God equips us for ministry to others as we study and struggle to know Him. We are not simply filling our heads with information. What we learn about Jesus changes our hearts and translates into ministry to others.

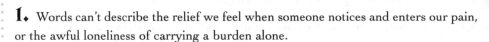

1. Words can't describe the relief we feel when someone notices and enters our pain, or the awful loneliness of carrying a burden alone.

2. The Passover that is only days away will be remembered as the Last Supper. Jesus' enemies are plotting His death, and He is running out of time.

3. If you've ever felt slightly depressed at a party, you'll have some idea of how Jesus felt. His closest friends wanted a military/political messiah to overthrow the Romans. Jesus tried to explain His mission (Matthew 20:18–21; Luke 9:44–46), but they had other matters on their minds and couldn't digest what He was saying.

4. Nard is an expensive perfume, imported from India. The ancients poured nard on a corpse as part of the burial process. Aromas often have strong associations. This well-known fragrance was associated with death. Mary's actions were as blatant as visiting a dying person and talking about funeral arrangements.

5. The disciples were concerned about money and waste. They were detached from what Jesus was facing.

6. Some believe this was a lavish gift, a gesture of love and worship (which it certainly was), but that Mary didn't understand the greater significance of her anointing. But she had been His student. She heard Him explain His mission. She experienced His compassion and empathy when her brother died. She saw Him raise her brother to life, so she had reason to believe Jesus would rise again too. Jesus defends her and explains the meaning of her actions. See also Matthew 26:6–13 and Mark 14:3–9.

7. Jesus' extraordinary words of praise indicate how deeply she had ministered to Him.

8. When Jesus wept with Mary over Lazarus' death, she learned that a true image bearer enters the struggles of others. Jesus faces the Cross. His disciples are in denial. Mary comes alongside. She affirms the path Jesus has chosen and encourages Him to obey His Father. It is a sacred moment and a strong example for us.

✦DIGGING DEEPER✦

Exodus 17:9–12   <u>Aaron and Hur give strength to Moses.</u>

Ruth 1:16–17   <u>Ruth lays down her life for her bereft mother-in-law.</u>

1 Samuel 20:13   <u>Jonathan protects and blesses David who fears for his life.</u>

Esther 4:14   <u>Mordecai challenges Esther to be strong for God's purposes.</u>

Philippians 1:3–5   <u>Paul and the Philippians (including women) spread the gospel.</u>

Chapter 8: Pursuing My Purpose Behind the Scenes

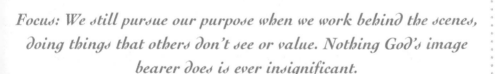

Focus: We still pursue our purpose when we work behind the scenes, doing things that others don't see or value. Nothing God's image bearer does is ever insignificant.

1. The world is full of unsung heroes. This is where God's value system clashes with how we value one another.

2. This story is actually more about Martha than Mary.

3. to **4.** These are opinion questions.

5. Martha was doing something important. But Jesus wanted her to see she was missing the most important thing. He leads Marys and Marthas to a common purpose — to know and live for Him.

6. Martha is one of six individuals in John's Gospel who confesses Jesus as the Son of God — Nathanael (1:49), Peter, (6:68–69), Martha (11:27), Thomas (20:28), John the apostle (20:30–31). Martha's faith in Jesus shines brightly in the darkness of this hour. She affirmed her faith in Jesus, even though He didn't save her brother from dying.

7. You can be sure Martha knew Mary had abandoned her again. Yet, this time she isn't asking Jesus to make Mary help her. Martha's relationship with Jesus has changed everything. Her heart is at peace. Her service matters to Him.

8. This is an opinion question.

✦ DIGGING DEEPER ✦

Once we grasp this amazing truth — that God sees me — it's hard to ever feel truly alone. This is one of the greatest comforts we can know.

Chapter 9: Living My Purpose in the Home

Focus: Hannah shows us how God works through mothers (and mentors) to shape the faith and beliefs of the next generation.

1. Our mothers remind us of our significant influence on future generations.

2. In Hannah's culture, the heartache of childlessness was compounded by the fact that a wife's duty was to bear sons for her husband. It was calamitous for a man to die without a son to carry on his name. Polygamy was considered an acceptable remedy for a first wife's barrenness. Elkanah exercised that option, intensifying Hannah's pain.

3. Although well-intentioned, Elkanah's words missed the mark and did nothing to lift Hannah's spirits. Instead of entering her struggle, he tried to coax her out of it. He missed an opportunity to join her in going deeper with God. Hannah went deeper alone. She will forge a Blessed Alliance with her son.

4. Twice we read that "The Lord had closed her womb." Hannah's struggle was with God, which gives Peninnah ammunition to torment her. Peninnah doesn't see the implications for herself.

5. Instead of acknowledging the repeated miracles that are taking place in her own body, Peninnah gloats over her successes and mocks Hannah for trusting God to no avail. Verse 6 tells us she essentially persecuted Hannah for trusting the LORD who had closed her womb.

6. Hannah's longing becomes so strong to see God's trustworthiness vindicated, she gives back the child she is dying to have.

7. Hannah's sufferings opened her eyes to see God's hand in all of life. She discovered God stands behind the ups and downs, the births and the barrenness of life. Though her heart ached over their separation, she trusted the God who held them in His hands. She learned through the heartache of infertility exactly what she needed to equip her child to become one of Israel's greatest leaders. Her theology steadied him through the rise and fall of Eli the priest, his own rejection when Israel demanded a king, King Saul's rise and fall, and David's torturous rise to power.

8. In biblical times, mothers weaned their children as late as three or four years old. While not a toddler, Samuel still was very young to be separated from his mother. It is remarkable that Hannah instilled so much in his heart in so brief a time.

✦ DIGGING DEEPER ✦

Here are some examples of Hannah's themes, which King David picks up:

- God is my rock and deliverer.
- God raises up and brings down.
- God gives victory and defeat in battle.
- God keeps the feet of His children secure—keeps them from falling.
- God gives strength and help to His anointed.

Chapter 10: Living My Purpose in the Church

Focus: Paul's relationship with the women of Philippi
reveals why the church needs our gifts and ministry.
The church can't be strong without us.

1. Most Christians have been blessed by the gifts and ministries of women.

2. Before Paul became a Christian he was a Pharisee — a religious purist who prided in (and paraded) his strict adherence to the Mosaic Law. Pharisees rigidly separated from anything or anyone (Gentiles, for example) that might taint their purity. Paul was so zealous, he persecuted Christians. Paul didn't detail his pedigree to brag or prove he was better than others, but to oppose false teachers who insisted Gentile believers must observe Jewish religious practices, when they only needed Christ.

3. Paul didn't act disappointed. He simply sat down and began teaching the women about Jesus.

4. Lydia was the first convert to Christ in Europe. She was a businesswoman with the means and courage to host the church in her home, despite the threat of violence.

5. Paul's stay in Philippi was cut short by violent opposition. Forced to leave, he surely worried over what would become of these new believers. But they were warriors. They spread the gospel in their city and pursued Paul with gifts and support. See Philippians 4:15–16.

6. Paul's warrior language underscores the urgency of our involvement in the cause of Christ. The church's mission is vast. Our Enemy fierce. Paul summons women to engage the battle with him.

7. Paul calls us to study and imitate Christ, by pouring out our lives for others. This is not a call to doormat living, but to costly, courageous living for God. Both Jesus and Paul stood up to wickedness. In this very letter, Paul is uncompromising in his rebuke of the false teachers. Sometimes imitating Christ means taking a bold stand.

8. The Blessed Alliance falls apart when everyone looks out for themselves. Paul urged putting others first and setting aside our differences for the sake of Christ. The metaphor of the body makes a lot of sense. We obsess over our bodies and want them to be healthy and strong. The church is the body of Christ. Jesus wants His body to be healthy, strong, and active too.

✦Digging Deeper✦

Our own bodies teach how important each of us is to the body of Christ. The slightest injury or malfunction in our bodies forces the rest of our bodies to compensate for the weakness. The body of Christ needs us to be strong in our relationship with God.

Chapter 11: Living My Purpose in the World

Focus: Abigail shows us how a woman pursues her purpose in the world. She defends the helpless, stands up for justice, and points God's people back to Him.

1. Throughout history, women have played powerful roles on the world's stage.

2.

	Nabal	David
Who?	Wealthy landowner in Carmel who had very large herds	David, God's anointed, who had been driven into the wilderness by a jealous King Saul
Relationship to Abigail?	Abigail's husband	Protector of her husband's flocks, a threat to her family and servants, and her future king
Character?	surly and mean	Gracious in protecting local herds from robbers and with a strong expectation of just treatment for his kindness
Mood?	Rude, dismissive, and ungrateful	Outraged by Nabal's injustice
Motive?	Selfishness and greed	Revenge

3. Eugene Peterson described the ancient wilderness as "a high-crime district." On the run from King Saul, David and his 400 mighty men retreated to the Judean wilderness where they voluntarily protected herdsmen in the area from robbers, including Nabal's flocks. In response, Nabal treated them with contempt, dismissing his indebtedness to them.

4. Remember, in the ancient culture women usually remained secluded and didn't interact publicly with men.

5. If Abigail had remained passive, many innocent lives would have been lost. God's honor was at stake because David was planning to take revenge, instead of trusting God to take up his cause.

6. Abigail can't reason with her husband—a sober reminder that it isn't always possible for a woman to be in a Blessed Alliance with her husband. But Abigail can reason with David, who shares her heart for God.

7. Abigail displays extraordinary courage and integrity in taking risks and in going home to face her husband.

8. This is an opinion question.

✦DIGGING DEEPER✦

Abigail's example helps us see there are opportunities right in front of us to take risks and take up the cause of those who are in need and to influence others to do what honors God.

Chapter 12: Awakening the Warrior in Me

Focus: Our efforts to understand God's purpose for us are incomplete until we take our purpose into our private lives.

1. This will help us all get personal with our purpose.

2.

1   Let us throw off everything that hinders and the sin that so easily entangles.

2   Let us run with perseverance the race marked out for us.

3   Let us fix our eyes on Jesus, the Author and Perfecter of our faith.

3. This is an opinion question.

4. Unbelief brought down Eve and Adam. It threatened to trip up Mary and Martha when their brother died. Hannah, Lydia, and Abigail ran with firm footsteps because they threw off fear and unbelief and trusted in their God. But trust isn't a feeling. Trust is confidence in someone you know, even when you don't understand what He is doing.

5. Think of the effort and stamina a marathon requires. God calls us to exert that same all-out effort in running the race He marked out for us and not to give up when we're ready to drop.

6. We can run because God is in control, working everything for our good and His glory—in the mess, the chaos, and the ordinariness of our private lives. His smile rests upon His daughters as we run by faith and live our purpose each day.

7. We fix our eyes on Jesus by getting to know Him in His Word and by telling ourselves the truth about Him as we run.

8. We are part of a vast company of believers—each one running in our moment in history. We are not alone. And everything we do counts.

✦ DIGGING DEEPER ✦

We will never discover all there is to know about Jesus. He came to show us the Father. He is the clearest picture of what God is like. Through His life and death, He revealed God's heart for us. As God's perfect image bearer, Jesus shows us what God created us to become. We are called to become like Jesus.

✦ABOUT THE AUTHOR✦

Carolyn Custis James (M.A. in Biblical Studies) is a vibrant new voice with a biblical and affirming message for women. Her vision is eloquently and passionately articulated in her books, *When Life and Beliefs Collide: How Knowing God Makes a Difference* (Zondervan, 2001), *Lost Women of The Bible: Finding Strength and Significance Through Their Stories* (Zondervan, 2005) and *Understanding Purpose,* (Thomas Nelson, 2006). Her next book, *Ruth—Loving God Enough to Break the Rules,* is scheduled for release in 2007.

Carolyn is the president of *WhitbyForum,* a ministry dedicated to helping women go deeper in their relationship with God and serve Him alongside their Christian brothers. She is a popular speaker at church conferences, colleges and other Christian organizations both in the US and abroad. She also serves as a visiting lecturer at theological seminaries, as a consulting editor for *Zondervan's Exegetical Commentary Series on the New Testament,* as well as a biblical consultant for the *Jesus Film for Women.* More recently, she established the *Synergy* conferences—a national gathering of women in seminary and in vocational ministries—in partnership with Reformed Theological Seminary and Campus Crusade for Christ International.

A pastor's daughter, Carolyn grew up in Portland, Oregon. During the years between her graduate education and her present ministries, she was a software developer and had her own business in Oxford, England. She and her husband Frank (President of Reformed Theological Seminary/Orlando) live in Orlando, Florida. They have one college-age daughter.

✦ Notes ✦

✦ Notes ✦

✦ NOTES ✦

✦ NOTES ✦

✦ NOTES ✦

✦ Notes ✦

THE COMPLETE WOMEN OF FAITH®
STUDY GUIDE SERIES

WOMEN OF FAITH
STUDY GUIDE SERIES

To find these and other inspirational products visit your local Christian retailer.

www.thomasnelson.com

OTHER SELECTIONS FOR WOMEN OF FAITH

Best-Selling authors and Women of Faith® speakers Patsy Clairmont, Mary Graham, Barbara Johnson, Marilyn Meberg, Grammy Award Winning singer Sandi Patty, Luci Swindoll, Sheila Walsh, Thelma Wells and dramatist Nicole Johnson bring humor and insight to women's daily lives. Sit back, exhale, and enjoy spending some time with these extraordinary women!

AVAILABLE WHEREVER BOOKS ARE SOLD.

THOMASNELSON.COM | WOMENOFFAITH.COM

W PUBLISHING GROUP
A Division of Thomas Nelson Publishers
Since 1798
wpublishinggroup.com

NELSON BOOKS
A Division of Thomas Nelson Publishers
Since 1798
thomasnelson.com

WOMEN OF FAITH
womenoffaith.com

COUNTRYMAN
A Division of Thomas Nelson Publishers
Since 1798
thomasnelson.com

HALF THE CHURCH

Recapturing
GOD'S GLOBAL VISION
for Women

CAROLYN CUSTIS JAMES

Carolyn Custis James presents an inspiring vision of God's plan for women that avoids assuming for them a particular social location or family situation. She reveals the surprising way God crafts a new identity for women who respond to the call of his kingdom — regardless of age, life stage, social location, and point on the globe.

Hardcover, Jacketed: 978-0-310-32556-7

Available in stores and online!

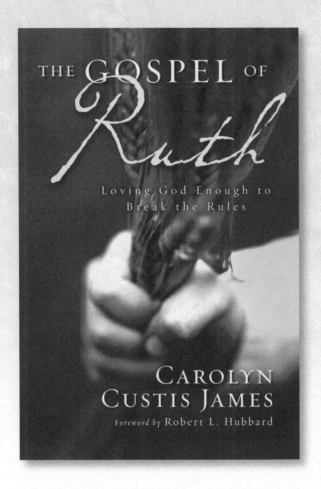

THE GOSPEL OF

Ruth

Loving God Enough to
Break the Rules

CAROLYN
CUSTIS JAMES

Foreword by Robert L. Hubbard